TIME FOR KIDS READERS

Our HOLIDAYS

by Elena Martin

Harcourt
SCHOOL PUBLISHERS

Orlando   Austin   New York   San Diego   Toronto   London

Visit *The Learning Site!*
www.harcourtschool.com

Holidays are important times.

REMEMBER KINGS DREAMS!!

Martin Luther King, Jr.
Civil Rights Leader
1929-1968

Some holidays are for remembering **important people**.

Some holidays are for remembering **Presidents**.

Some holidays are for remembering **heroes**.

Some holidays are for our **country**.

Some holidays have **parades**.

Some holidays are for **sharing**.